ANIMAL BATTLES

FENNEC FOX VS. SAND CAT

BY NATHAN SOMMER

TORQUE

BELLWETHER MEDIA • MINNEAPOLIS, MN

Torque brims with excitement perfect for thrill-seekers of all kinds. Discover daring survival skills, explore uncharted worlds, and marvel at mighty engines and extreme sports. In *Torque* books, anything can happen. Are you ready?

This edition first published in 2026 by Bellwether Media, Inc.

No part of this publication may be reproduced in whole or in part without written permission of the publisher. For information regarding permission, write to Bellwether Media, Inc., Attention: Permissions Department, 3500 American Blvd W, Suite 150, Bloomington, MN 55431.

Library of Congress Cataloging-in-Publication Data

LC record for Fennec Fox vs. Sand Cat
available at: https://lccn.loc.gov/2025012865

Text copyright © 2026 by Bellwether Media, Inc. TORQUE and associated logos are trademarks and/or registered trademarks of Bellwether Media, Inc. Bellwether Media is a division of FlutterBee Education Group.

Editor: Suzane Nguyen　　Designer: Josh Brink

Printed in the United States of America, North Mankato, MN.

TABLE OF CONTENTS

THE COMPETITORS	4
SECRET WEAPONS	10
ATTACK MOVES	16
READY, FIGHT!	20
GLOSSARY	22
TO LEARN MORE	23
INDEX	24

THE COMPETITORS

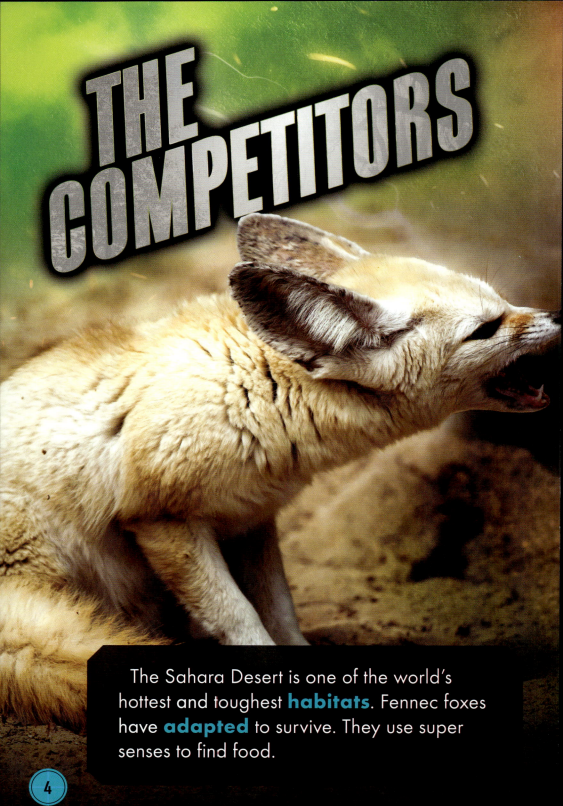

The Sahara Desert is one of the world's hottest and toughest **habitats**. Fennec foxes have **adapted** to survive. They use super senses to find food.

Fennec foxes share habitats with sand cats. Do not be fooled by these small cats. They can take down some deadly **predators**. But which small desert predator is tougher?

FENNEC FOX PROFILE

LENGTH
UP TO 24 INCHES
(61 CENTIMETERS)

WEIGHT
UP TO 3.5 POUNDS
(1.6 KILOGRAMS)

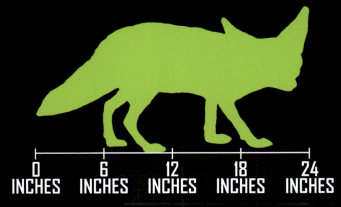

HABITATS

DESERTS

SHRUBLANDS

FENNEC FOX RANGE

RANGE

Fennec foxes are the world's smallest foxes. They have thick, cream-colored fur and long, bushy tails with black tips. The foxes have large, batlike ears. These can grow up to 6 inches (15.2 centimeters) long!

Fennec foxes like to live in deserts and shrublands. The foxes are active at night. They spend all day in **burrows**.

BURROW

SOCIAL FOXES

Fennec foxes live in groups of up to 10 members. They talk by barking and growling.

Sand cats are one of the smallest wild cats. The cats grow up to 36.5 inches (92.7 centimeters) long from head to tail. The cats have sandy, grayish fur. They have short legs and long tails. Large, pointed ears sit on their wide heads.

Sand cats are found in the deserts of North Africa and central Asia. The cats live alone in burrows or dens.

LENGTHY TAILS

Sand cats' tails can grow longer than half of their body length.

SAND CAT PROFILE

LENGTH
UP TO 36.5 INCHES
(92.7 CENTIMETERS)

WEIGHT
UP TO 7.5 POUNDS
(3.4 KILOGRAMS)

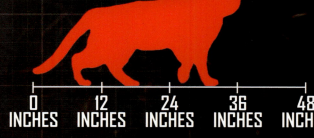

0 INCHES 12 INCHES 24 INCHES 36 INCHES 48 INCHES

HABITATS

 SHRUBLANDS

 DESERTS

SAND CAT RANGE

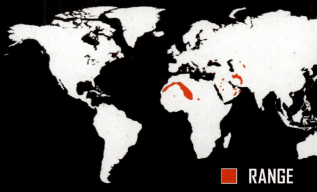

■ RANGE

SECRET WEAPONS

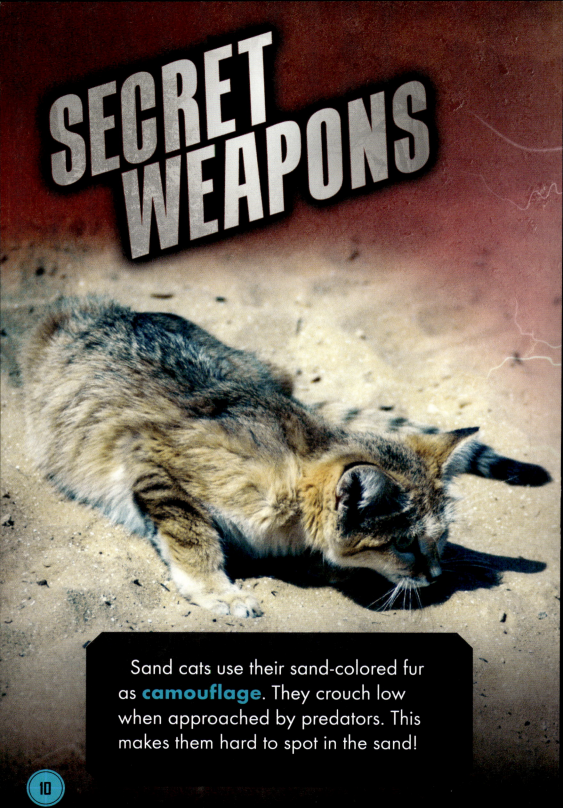

Sand cats use their sand-colored fur as **camouflage**. They crouch low when approached by predators. This makes them hard to spot in the sand!

FENNEC FOX LEAPING DISTANCE

SURFBOARD
8 FEET (2.4 METERS)

FENNEC FOX
4 FEET (1.2 METERS)

0 FEET | 2 FEET | 4 FEET | 6 FEET | 8 FEET

Fennec foxes have powerful legs. They can leap up to 4 feet (1.2 meters) in one jump! The foxes can also run at speeds of up to 20 miles (32.2 kilometers) per hour.

Large ears give fennec foxes top-notch hearing. The foxes can hear **prey** moving under the sand. Their ears also help cool them down in extreme heat.

SAND CAT CANINE TOOTH SIZE

UP TO 0.4 INCHES (1 CENTIMETER)

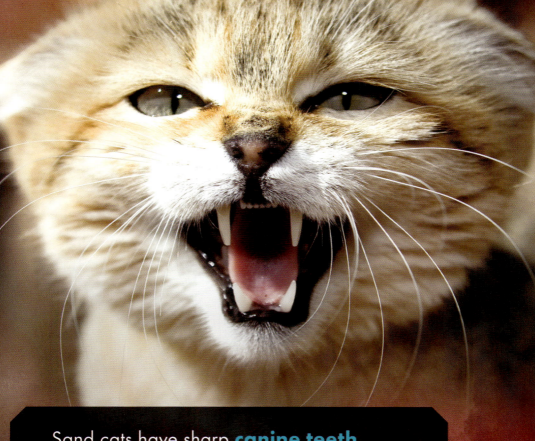

Sand cats have sharp **canine teeth**. They use these to deliver deadly bites to prey. The teeth also help the cats defend themselves against predators.

SECRET WEAPONS

FENNEC FOX

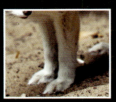
POWERFUL LEGS

LARGE EARS

FURRY FEET

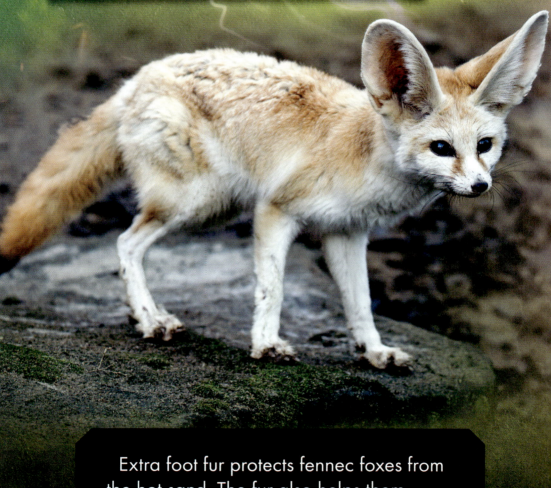

Extra foot fur protects fennec foxes from the hot sand. The fur also helps them walk on loose sand. They can chase prey without slipping.

SECRET WEAPONS

SAND CAT

CAMOUFLAGE

SHARP CANINE TEETH

SHOVEL-LIKE PAWS

Sand cats are excellent diggers. They dig up prey from under the sand with their shovel-like paws. The cats also use their paws to strike enemies.

ATTACK MOVES

Fennec foxes hunt lizards, **insects**, and small **mammals**. They sit quietly listening for prey beneath the sand. Once prey is found, they use all four legs to dig up their meals!

DESERT DIET

Fennec foxes can survive on little water. They get most of their water from plants they eat.

Sand cats are **opportunistic** eaters. They mostly hunt **rodents** buried underground. The cats use good hearing to find food. Then they attack!

Fennec foxes leap on prey. They jump high and pounce on prey feet first. This allows them to defeat animals like rabbits and birds that are larger than them.

HIDDEN MEALS

Sand cats often bury larger prey under sand. This allows them to save food for later.

Sand cats are brave hunters. They are known to hunt **venomous** snakes. The cats weaken snakes with multiple blows to the head. Then they defeat the snakes with deadly bites!

READY, FIGHT!

A sand cat listens for prey under the sand. Suddenly, a fennec fox pounces on it from behind. The sand cat throws the fox off its back.

The sand cat strikes the fox's head with its paws. It defeats the weakened fox by biting its neck. The wild cat survived today's surprise attack!

GLOSSARY

adapted—changed over a long period of time

burrows—tunnels or holes in the ground used as animal homes

camouflage—colors and patterns used to help an animal hide in its surroundings

canine teeth—long, pointed teeth that are often the sharpest in the mouth

habitats—the homes or areas where animals prefer to live

insects—small animals with six legs and hard outer bodies; an insect's body is divided into three parts.

mammals—warm-blooded animals that have backbones and feed their young milk

opportunistic—taking advantage of a situation

predators—animals that hunt other animals for food

prey—animals that are hunted by other animals for food

rodents—small animals that gnaw on their food; mice, rats, and squirrels are all rodents.

venomous—able to produce venom; venom is a kind of poison made by some snakes.

TO LEARN MORE

AT THE LIBRARY

Fabiny, Sarah. *Where Is the Sahara Desert?* New York, N.Y.: Penguin Workshop, 2023.

Sommer, Nathan. *Red Fox vs. Fisher*. Minneapolis, Minn.: Bellwether Media, 2024.

Woodward, John. *Life Underground: Tunnel Into a World of Wildlife*. New York, N.Y.: DK Publishing, 2023.

ON THE WEB

Factsurfer.com gives you a safe, fun way to find more information.

1. Go to www.factsurfer.com

2. Enter "fennec fox vs. sand cat" into the search box and click 🔍.

3. Select your book cover to see a list of related content.

INDEX

adapted, 4
Asia, 8
attack, 17, 20
bites, 13, 19, 20
burrows, 7, 8
camouflage, 10
canine teeth, 13
color, 7, 8, 10
dens, 8
dig, 15, 16
ears, 7, 8, 12
fur, 7, 8, 10, 14
habitats, 4, 5, 6, 7, 8, 9
hearing, 12, 17
hunt, 16, 17, 19
leap, 11, 18

legs, 8, 11, 16
North Africa, 8
opportunistic, 17
paws, 15, 20
pounce, 18, 20
predators, 5, 10, 13
prey, 12, 13, 14, 15, 16, 17, 18, 19, 20
range, 4, 6, 8, 9
size, 5, 6, 7, 8, 9, 12, 13
speed, 11
tails, 7, 8
water, 16
weapons, 14, 15

The images in this book are reproduced through the courtesy of: Arco / G. Lacz/ Alamy, front cover (sand cat head hero), pp. 2-3 (sand cat face), 15 (sharp canine teeth), 20-24 (sand cat face); Vladimir Wrangel, front cover (fennec fox hero), pp. 4, 14 (powerful legs); Shams F Amir, front cover (fennec fox eyes); Alexandr Junek Imaging, front cover (sand cat body); Jearu, pp. 2-3, 20-24 (fennec fox); DKeith, pp. 2-3, 20-24 (sand cat body); Alain Dragesco-Joffe/ Alamy, pp. 5, 15, 19; Konrad Wothe/ Alamy, pp. 6-7, 13; Yair Leibovich, pp. 8-9; Payman sazesh/ Wikipedia Commons, p. 9; David Hosking/ Alamy, p. 10; Floridapfe from S.Korea Kim in cherl/ Getty Images, p. 11; Martin Mecnarowski, p. 12; imageBROKER.com, p. 14 (large ears); novazai, p. 14 (furry feet); Stanislav Duben, p. 14; Christian Hütter/ Alamy, p. 15 (camouflage); cgwp.co.uk/ Alamy, p. 15 (shovel-like paws); Vine.Photographic, p. 16; CTK Photo/Igor Zehl/ Alamy, p. 17; Bernard Bailorucki/ Alamy, p. 18.